VITALIS

**BIBLIOTHECA
BOHEMICA**

Letter
to Father

Franz Kafka's father, Herrmann

Franz Kafka

Letter to Father

Vitalis

© Vitalis, Praha 2004

Translation: Karen Reppin
Editors: Marc Reppin, Siegfried Mortkowitz
Cover illustration: Karel Hruška
Printed by Finidr, Český Těšín
All rights reserved.

ISBN 80-85938-29-4

www.vitalis-verlag.com

Dearest Father,

You once asked me recently why I claim to be afraid of you. I did not know, as usual, what to answer, partly out of my fear of you and partly because the cause of this fear consists of too many details for me to put even halfway into words. And if I try to answer you in writing here, it will be only very incomplete anyway, because even in writing my fear and its consequences inhibit me toward you, and because the magnitude of the material far exceeds my memory and my understanding.

To you the matter always appeared to be very simple, at least to the extent you spoke about it in front of me and, indiscriminately, in front of many others. It seemed to you more or less like this: you have worked hard your entire life, sacrificing everything for your children, especially me; as a result, I have lived "like a lord," have had complete freedom to study whatever I wanted, and have had no cause for material worries, indeed for worries of any kind at all; you demanded no gratitude for that – you know "the gratitude of children" – but still expected at least some sort of cooperation, some sign of sympathy; instead I have always hidden from you in my room, among my books, with crazy friends[1], in extrava-

---

[1] Besides Max Brod (1884–1968), the Eastern Jewish actor Jizchak Löwy (1887–1942), who performed with his ensemble in Yiddish and also wrote his own stories, also belonged to Franz Kafka's circle of friends.

gant ideas; I have never spoken to you openly, I never came to you in the synagogue, I never visited you in Franzensbad², nor otherwise showed any sense of family, I never took an interest in the shop or any other concerns of yours, I saddled you with the factory and then deserted you, I encouraged Ottla in her obstinacy, and while I don't lift a finger for you (I don't even get you a theatre ticket), I do everything for friends. Were you to sum up your judgement of me, then it turns out that you do not actually reproach me for anything really improper or evil (with the exception, perhaps, of my latest marriage plan), but for coldness, reserve, ingratitude. And, what is more, you reproach me for it in such a way as if it were my fault, as if I might have been able, with the mere turn of a wheel, to arrange everything differently, while you were not in the slightest bit at fault, except perhaps for having been too good to me.

This, your usual portrayal, I regard as correct only to the extent that I also believe that you are entirely blameless for our estrangement. But just as entirely blameless am I. If I could get you to acknowledge this, then what would be possible is not a new life – for this we are both much too old – but still a kind of peace, not a cessation but still a mitigation of your incessant reproaches.

Strangely enough, you have some notion of what I mean. Thus, for example, you recently said to me: "I have always been fond of you even if on the surface I

Brod promoted Kafka's literary inclinations, Löwy awakened his interest in Orthodox Judaism. Hermann Kafka looked upon his son's activity in both these areas unfavourably since, in his opinion, it distracted Franz from the more important things in life (striving for economic success and social recognition).

² Kafka's parents frequently spent their holidays at this north Bohemian spa.

have not been toward you as other fathers tend to be, precisely because I cannot play a part as others can." Now, Father, I have on the whole never doubted your kindness toward me, but this remark I consider incorrect. You cannot play a part, it is true, but merely for this reason to want to claim that other fathers play a part is either a mere know-it-all attitude beyond further discussion, or perhaps – and this is, in my opinion, what it really is – a veiled expression for there being something wrong between us, and that you have played your part in bringing it about, though without being at fault. If you really mean this, then we agree.

Of course, I am not saying that I have become what I am only as a result of your influence. That would be very much an exaggeration (and, in fact, I lean toward this exaggeration). It is quite possible that even if I had grown up entirely free of your influence, I could still not have become a person after your own heart. I would probably still have become a weakly, timid, hesitant, restless person, neither Robert Kafka nor Karl Hermann,[3] but still very different from what I really am, and we would have got on with each other excellently. I would have been happy to have you as a friend, boss, uncle, grandfather, yes even (though rather more hesitantly) as a father-in-law. It is only as a father that you were too strong for me, especially since my brothers died young, my sisters only arrived much later, so that I had to endure the first knock or two all alone, and for that I was much too weak.

---

[3] Robert Kafka, son of Hermann Kafka's brother Philipp, was an energetic and professionally successful man. Kafka's eldest sister, Elli (born 1889), was married to Karl Hermann, who resembled Kafka's father in nature and build and was likewise an industrious businessman.

Compare the two of us: I, to put it very briefly, a Löwy with a certain Kafka foundation[4] that, however, just isn't set in motion by the Kafka will to life, business and conquest, but by a Löwy spur that operates more secretively, more timidly, and in a different direction, and which often fails to work at all. You, on the other hand, a true Kafka in strength, health, appetite, loudness of voice, eloquence, self-satisfaction, worldly superiority, stamina, presence of mind, knowledge of human nature, a certain generosity; of course, also with all the failings and weaknesses that go with these advantages, into which your temperament and sometimes your violent temper drive you. You are perhaps not entirely a Kafka in your general world view, in so far as I can compare you to Uncle Philipp, Ludwig and Heinrich. That is strange, and here I don't see quite clearly, either. Surely, they were all more cheerful, fresher, more casual, more easygoing, less severe than you. (In this, by the way, I have inherited a lot from you and have taken much too good care of this inheritance, though without having the necessary counterbalance in my nature, as you have.) On the other hand, you too have in this regard undergone various phases, you were perhaps more cheerful before your children, especially I, disappointed and depressed you at home (when strangers came, you were quite different), and you have perhaps become more cheerful again now that your grandchildren and your son-in-law give you some of the warmth your children, with the exception perhaps of Valli[5], could not give you. In any case, we were so different and in this difference so dangerous to

---

[4] The Löwys are Kafka's maternal ancestors; here he is addressing the blending of contradictory hereditary features in his genealogy. The Löwys represent sensitivity and intelligence; the Kafkas, aggressive business acumen.

[5] Valli (Valerie, born 1890) was Kafka's second-eldest sister.

each other that, had anyone wanted to figure out in advance how I, the slowly developing child, and you, the completed man, would behave toward one another, he could have presumed that you would simply trample me into the ground until nothing remained of me. Now, that did not happen, what lives cannot be calculated, but perhaps something more terrible happened. In saying this I continue to beg you not to forget that I never, not in the slightest, believe in any guilt on your part. The effect you had on me was the effect you had to have, but you should stop taking it as particular malice on my part that I succumbed to your influence.

I was a fearful child; in spite of this, I was certainly also obstinate, as children are; mother certainly spoiled me too, but I cannot believe that I was terribly difficult to handle, I cannot believe that a friendly word, a quiet taking by the hand, a kind look, could not have got me to do anything that was wanted of me. Now, you are basically a kind and soft-hearted person (what follows does not contradict this, I am speaking only of the image through which you influenced the child), but not every child has the perseverance and the courage to go on searching until it comes upon this kindness. You can only treat a child as you yourself are constituted, with strength, noise and violent temper, and, what is more, in this case it seemed to you extremely suitable because you wanted me to be a strong, brave boy.

Your child-rearing methods in the very early years I cannot, of course, directly describe today, but I can more or less imagine them by the conclusions I drew of later years, and by your treatment of Felix[6]. Here one must emphasize the fact that you were younger then and

[6] Felix (1911–1940) and Gerti (1912–1972) were the children of Elli and Karl Hermann.

therefore livelier, wilder, more natural, even more carefree than you are today, and that you were completely tied to the shop besides, hardly able to be with me once a day and therefore making all the more profound an impression on me, which never really paled into an habituation.

I remember directly only one incident from the early years. Perhaps you remember it, too. One night I kept on whimpering for water, certainly not because I was thirsty, but probably partly to be annoying, partly to amuse myself. After several strong threats had not helped, you took me out of bed, carried me out onto the pavlatche[7] and left me standing there alone for a little while in my nightshirt outside the locked door. I do not want to say that this was wrong, perhaps there was really no other way at the time to acquire peace and quiet that night, but I only want to characterize by this your child-rearing methods and their effect on me. After that I was really quite obedient, but I came away from it with internal damage. What was for me self-evident, my pointless asking for water, and the extreme terror of being carried outside were two things that I, my nature being what it was, could never properly connect. Even years afterward I still suffered from the tormenting fancy that that enormous man, my father, the ultimate authority, could for almost no reason come during the night and take me out of bed and carry me out onto the pavlatche, and that meant that I was a mere nothing to him.

This was, at the time, only a small beginning, but this feeling of nothingness that often overwhelms me (a feeling, however, also noble and fruitful in other respects)

---

[7] Enclosed galleries on the inner courtyards of Prague apartment buildings which connected several apartments.

stems largely from your influence. I would have needed a little encouragement, a little friendliness, a little keeping open of my path; instead you obstructed it for me, with the good intention, it is true, of making me take a different path. But for that I was useless. You encouraged me, for example, when I saluted and marched smartly, but I was no future soldier, or you encouraged me when I could eat heartily or even drink beer with my meal, or when I could repeat songs I did not understand, or repeat after you your favorite sayings, but none of this had anything to do with my future. And it is characteristic that even today you really only encourage me in something when you yourself are involved in it, when it is your sense of self which I injure (for example, by my intended marriage[8]) or which is injured in me (for example, when Pepa[9] is abusive to me). Then I am encouraged, reminded of my worth, shown the matches that I would be entitled to make, and Pepa is completely condemned. But apart from the fact that at my present age I am already almost impervious to encouragement, what help would it be to me anyway if it only occurred when it does not concern me in the first place?

At that time, and whenever possible at that time, I could have used some encouragement. I was, after all, already weighed down by your sheer physical presence. I remember, for example, how we often undressed to-

---

[8] Kafka's father had practical objections to his son's intentions to marry Felice Bauer (1887–1960): he feared financial burdens for his family. Kafka broke off the engagement in 1914 for psychological reasons, which he brings up elsewhere in *Letter to Father*. Kafka met his second fiancée, Julie Wohryzek (1891–1944), in 1919; she was rejected by Kafka's father because of her low social position. Kafka broke off this engagement in the summer of 1920 after meeting Milena Jesenská.

[9] Pet name for Josef Pallak (1882–1942), who married Kafka's sister Valli in 1913. He was not accepted by Hermann Kafka because he could not offer his wife the wished-for financial security.

gether in the same changing-room. I was skinny, weakly, slight; you were strong, tall, broad. Even in the changing-room I felt pitiful, and what's more, not only in your eyes, but in the eyes of the entire world, for you were for me the standard by which everything was measured. When we stepped out of the changing-room in front of everyone – I holding your hand, a small skeleton, insecure, barefoot on the planks, afraid of the water, incapable of copying your swimming strokes, which you, with good intentions but actually to my profound shame, kept on demonstrating to me – then at such moments I was full of despair and all my bad experiences in all areas tallied marvelously. I felt happiest when you sometimes undressed first and I could stay in the changing-room alone and postpone the shame of appearing in public until you at last came looking for me and drove me out of the changing-room. I was grateful to you that you did not appear to notice my anguish; I was proud, too, of my father's body. Incidentally, this difference between us still exists much the same today.

Further, this corresponded to your mental domination. You had worked your way up so far on nothing but your own strength, consequently you had unlimited confidence in your own opinion. This was not so dazzling for me as a child as it would be later for the maturing young man. From your easychair you ruled the world. Your opinion was right, every other was mad, eccentric, *meshugge*, not normal. In fact, your self-confidence was so great that you did not have to be consistent at all and still never ceased being right. It also happened on occasion that you had no opinion at all on a topic and consequently all opinions that were possible on this topic were necessarily, and without exception, wrong. You could, for instance, rail at the Czechs, then at the Germans, then at the Jews, and not only selectively but in every respect, and finally no one was left but you. For me, you took on that enigmatic something that all tyrants have whose law is founded on their person, not their reasoning. At least so it seemed to me.

Now, compared with me, you were indeed surprisingly often right; in conversation this was a matter of course, for there was hardly ever any conversation between us, but also in reality. But that was also nothing particularly incomprehensible: I stood, after all, in all of my thinking under your strong pressure, also in that thinking, and particularly in that, which did not correspond with yours. All these thoughts seemingly dependent on you were from the start burdened by your belittling judgement; it was almost impossible to endure it while elaborating a complete and lasting thought. I am not speaking here of some lofty thought, but of every small childhood undertaking. One had only to be happy about something or other, be wrapped up in it, come home and express it, and the answer was a sarcastic sigh, a shaking of the head, a finger-tapping on the table: "Is that all it is?" or, "Such worries you have," or, "What you have time to think about," or, "What can you buy with that?" or, "Big deal!" Naturally one couldn't expect enthusiasm from you for every childish triviality when you lived in a state of worry and trouble. But that was not the point, either. The point was much more that you always and inevitably had to cause the child such disappointments by virtue of your antagonistic nature and, furthermore, that this antagonism, through the accumulation of material, was continuously reinforced so that it eventually asserted itself out of habit, even if for once you were of the same opinion as I, and finally that these disappointments of the child were not the ordinary disappointments of life but, since they concerned you, the authority on everything, struck at the very heart of things. Courage, determination, confidence, delight in this and that did not last to the end when you were against it or even if your opposition could only be assumed; and it could well be assumed with just about everything I did.

This applied to thoughts as well as to people. It was enough that I was a little interested in someone – which did not happen so often, given my nature – for you to interfere with insults, defamation, and degradation, without any consideration of my feelings or respect for my judgement. Innocent, childlike people such as, for example, the Yiddish actor Löwy had to pay for it. Without knowing him you compared him, in a dreadful way which I've already forgotten, to vermin and, as was so often the case with the people I liked, you automatically had that proverb of the dogs and the fleas at hand.[10] Here I particularly remember that actor because I made a note of your remarks about him at the time with the comment: "My father speaks about my friend (whom he doesn't even know) this way simply because he is my friend. I will always be able to hold this against him when he accuses me of lacking a child's love and gratitude." What was always incomprehensible to me was your utter lack of sensitivity to the kind of suffering and shame you could inflict on me with your words and judgements; it was as if you had no notion of your power. I, too, must surely have often hurt you with words, but then I always knew it, it pained me, but I could not control myself, I could not hold the word back, I regretted it even as I was saying it. But you lashed out with

[10] Löwy was one of Kafka's "crazy friends" (see note 1). The proverb Kafka refers to here is: "He who lies down with dogs gets up with fleas."

your words without hesitation, you felt sorry for no one, neither during nor afterwards, one was absolutely defenseless against you.

But your whole method of upbringing was like this. I think you have a gift for bringing up children; in this upbringing you could certainly have used a person like yourself; he would have seen the sense of what you told him, would not have bothered about anything else and would quietly have done as he was told. For me as a child, however, everything that you shouted at me was virtually a commandment from heaven, I never forgot it, it stayed with me as the most important means for judging the world, above all for judging you yourself, and in this you failed completely. Since as a child I was with you mainly at mealtimes, your lessons were for the most part lessons on correct table manners. Whatever was brought to the table had to be eaten up, the quality of the meal was not to be discussed – you, however, often found the meal inedible; called it "this slop"; the "animal" (the cook) had spoiled it. Because you, in accordance with your strong appetite and your particular predilection, ate everything quickly, hot and in big mouthfuls, the child had to hurry, there was a gloomy silence at the table, interrupted by admonitions: "First eat, then speak," or, "Faster, faster, faster," or, "You see, I've long since finished." We were not allowed to chew bones, you were. We were not allowed to slurp vinegar, you were. The main thing was that the bread be cut straight; but that you did it with a knife dripping with gravy was immaterial. We had to pay attention not to let any scraps fall onto the floor, in the end most of the scraps were under you. At the table we were only allowed to eat, but you cleaned and clipped your fingernails, sharpened pencils, cleaned your ears with a toothpick. Please understand me correctly, Father: in themselves these would have been utterly insignificant details, they only became depressing for me because you, the toweringly authoritative person for me, never held yourself to the commandments you imposed on me. This is how the world came to be divided into three parts for me, one in which I, the slave, lived under laws that had been invented only for me and moreover which I could, I didn't know why, never fully comply with, then a second world, infinitely distant from mine, in which you lived, preoccupied with government, with the issuing of orders and with the annoyance at their not being obeyed, and finally a third world wherein everyone else lived happily and free from orders and from having to obey. I was forever in disgrace: either I obeyed your orders, that was a disgrace, for they were, after all, meant only for me; or I was defiant, that was also a disgrace, for how dare I defy you; or I could not obey because I didn't have, for example, your strength, your appetite, your skill, even though you expected it of me as a matter of course; and that was the greatest disgrace of all. In this way moved not the thoughts but the feelings of the child.

My situation at that time becomes clearer perhaps if I compare it with that of Felix. Yes, you treat him similarly, you even employ a particularly terrible child-rearing method against him in that whenever he does something during the meal that is in your opinion unclean, you are not content with saying, as you used to say to me, "You are a disgusting pig," but add, "A thorough Hermann," or, "Just like your father." Now perhaps – more than "perhaps" one cannot say – this doesn't really hurt Felix a great deal since you are only a grandfather to him, albeit an especially important one, but still not everything as you were to me; besides, Felix is a quiet, already to some extent manly personality, who perhaps allows himself to be taken in, but not permanently influenced by, a thunderous voice, above all, however, he is still only relatively seldom with you and is influenced by other things, you are for him a rather dear curiosity from which he can select whatever he wants. For me you were not at all a curiosity, I could not choose, I had to take everything.

And this without being able to say anything against it, for right from the outset it is not possible for you to speak calmly about a subject you do not agree with or that wasn't initiated by you; your imperious temperament does not allow it. In recent years you have been excusing this with your nervous heart, I didn't know that you had ever been essentially different, at most your nervous heart is a means for you to impose your dominance more rigorously, as the thought of it necessarily smothers the least opposition from others. This is, of course, no accusation, only the establishment of a fact. As with Ottla[11]: You say, "One cannot talk to her at all, she immediately pounces on you," but in reality she doesn't begin by pouncing at all; you mistake the person for the topic; the topic pounces on you and right away, without listening to the person, you make up your mind about it, whatever is still said afterwards can only irritate you further, never convince you. Then one only hears from you: "Do what you want; as far as I'm concerned you are free; you are of age, I have no advice to give you," and all this with that terrible hoarse undertone of anger and abso-

---

[11] Ottla, really Ottilie (born 1892), was the youngest of Kafka's three sisters. With her he felt related in character; he supported her in her attempts to emancipate herself professionally and in her right to choose her husband herself, even if against her father's will.

lute condemnation which makes me tremble less today than during my childhood only because the child's exclusive sense of guilt has been partly replaced by insight into our helplessness, yours and mine.

The impossibility of peaceful communication had yet another, actually very natural, consequence: I lost the ability to speak. I wouldn't have become such an eloquent speaker in any case, to be sure, but I would still have had the usual fluency of everyday human language under control. But already very early on you forbade me to speak; your threat, "Not a word of contradiction!" and the raised hand that accompanied it have been with me since that time. I acquired in your presence – you are, as soon as it concerns your own matters, an excellent speaker – a hesitant, stammering manner of speaking, and even that was too much for you, eventually I kept silent, at first perhaps out of spite, and later because I could neither think nor speak in your presence. And because you were the one who actually raised me, this continued to affect me throughout my life. It is really a peculiar error for you to think that I have never been obedient to you. "Always against everything" is really not my life's principle toward you, as you believe and reproach me for. On the contrary: had I obeyed you less, you would certainly be more pleased with me. Instead, all your parental measures hit the mark; I could not avoid a single grip; I am the way I am (apart, of course, from the fundamentals and influence of life) as a result of your upbringing and my obedience. That this result is nevertheless embarrassing to you, indeed, that you unconsciously refuse to acknowledge it as the result of your upbringing, is because your hand and my material were so alien to one another. You would say: "Not a word of contradiction!" and wanted thereby to silence the disa-

greeable opposing forces in me; but this effect was too strong for me, I was too obedient, I fell completely silent, hid from you and dared to stir only when I was so far away from you that your power could no longer reach me, at least not directly. But you stood before it and it all seemed to you to be "contra" again, whereas it was only the inevitable consequence of your strength and my weakness.

Your extremely effective rhetorical child-rearing devices, which never failed with me, at least, were: abuse, threats, sarcasm, spiteful laughter and – strangely enough – self-pity.

I cannot remember your scolding me directly and with explicit abusive language. It wasn't really necessary, you had so many other means, and in conversation at home and particularly in the shop the words of abuse flew all around me and in such numbers onto other peoples' heads that as a small boy I was sometimes almost stunned by them and had no reason not to apply them to me, for the people you were abusing were certainly no worse than me, and you were certainly no more dissatisfied with them than with me. And even here was your puzzling innocence and unassailability again; you cursed without the slightest scruple, yet you condemned cursing in others and forbade it.

You reinforced the abuse with threats, and that applied to me, too. How terrible, for example, this was for me: "I'll tear you apart like a fish," even though I knew, of course, that nothing worse would follow (as a small child I didn't know this, however), but it corresponded almost exactly to my notions of your power that you would have been capable of this. It was terrible as well when you ran around the table yelling, to grab one of us, obviously not even wanting to grab, yet pretending to, and in the end Mother seemed to rescued one. Once again we had, it seemed to the child, remained alive by your mercy and carried on our lives as an undeserved gift from you. Here the threats about the consequences of disobedience can be mentioned, too. Whenever I started doing something you didn't like and you threatened me with the prospect of failure, my reverence for your opinion was so great that failure was, even if only at a later time, inevitable. I lost confidence in my own ability to act. I was unsteady, doubtful. The older I got, the more material you could hold against me as proof of my worthlessness; gradually, in a certain regard, you began really to be right. Once again I guard against claiming that I became like this only because of you; you only reinforced what was there, but you reinforced it greatly because you were very powerful in relation to me and you used all your power for that purpose.

You had a special confidence in bringing up children by means of irony, this was most in keeping with your superiority over me. An admonition from you usually took this form: "Can't you do it in such and such a way? It's already too much for you, isn't it? For that, you have no time, of course?" and the like. Every such question would be accompanied by malicious laughter and a malicious face. One was, as it were, already punished before even knowing one had done something bad. Provocative were also those rebukes in which one was treated as a third person, not even considered worthy of being angrily addressed; when you would speak formally to Mother, but actually to me, who was sitting right there, for example: "Of course, that is too much to expect of our worthy son," and the like. (This produced a corollary in that, for example, I didn't dare to ask you directly, and later, out of habit, didn't even think of asking you directly when Mother was around. It was much less dangerous for the child to put a question about you to Mother, sitting beside you; one asked Mother then: "How is Father?" and thus protected oneself against surprises.) There were, of course, also cases in which one very much agreed with the nastiest irony, namely, when it was directed at someone else, like Elli[12], with whom I was on bad terms for years. For me it was a feast of malice and gloating when, at every mealtime, such things were said of her as: "She should be sitting ten meters away from the table, the fat thing," and then, when from your easychair, malicious, without the slightest trace of friendliness or good humor, a bitter enemy, you extravagantly imitated the way she sat there and how utterly repulsive you found it. How often this and similar things had to be repeated, how little you actually achieved thereby. I think it was because the expenditure of rage and malice did not seem to be in proper relation to the matter itself, one did not have the feeling that this rage was generated by this trifling matter of sitting far from the table, but that it had existed in all its dimensions from the beginning and only by chance used in this matter as a pretext for breaking out. Since one was convinced that a pretext would be found anyway, one didn't try very hard, and one's feelings grew dulled from the constant threats; one had gradually become almost certain of not getting a beating, anyway. One became a sullen, inattentive, disobedient child, always on the run, mainly within myself. So you suffered, so we suffered. From your point of view you were absolutely right when, through clenched teeth and that gurgling laughter which gave the child its first ideas of hell, you used to say bit-

---

[12] Kafka's eldest sister (see note 2).

terly (as you did just recently about a letter from Constantinople[13]): "What a *great* bunch this is!"

What seemed absolutely incompatible with this attitude toward your children was when you complained publicly, which happened very often. I admit that as a child (but definitely later) I had no feeling for this and did not understand how you could possibly expect to get sympathy. You were so enormous in every respect; what could you gain from our pity or even our help? Actually, you necessarily had to scorn them, as you so often scorned us. I therefore did not believe the complaints and looked for some kind of secret intention behind them. Only later did I comprehend that you really suffered a great deal because of your children, but at that time, when the complaints might under different circumstances still have met with a childish, open mind, unhesitating, ready to help, to me they once again had to be an all-too-obvious means of rearing and humiliating me, as such not in themselves very strong, but with the harmful side-effect that the child got used to not taking seriously precisely those things it should have taken seriously.

Luckily, though, there were also exceptions to this, mostly when you suffered in silence, and love and kindness by their own strength overcame all obstacles and immediately seized hold of me. Rare as this was, it was wonderful. For instance, in earlier years, when I saw you after lunch on a hot summer afternoon, tired and taking a short nap at the office, your elbows on the desk, or when you joined us on the summer holidays, on Sundays, all tired out; or when Mother was gravely ill you held onto the bookcase, shaking with sobs; or when during my last illness you quietly came to see me in Ottla's

---

[13] This probably alludes to his father's business correspondence.

room, standing on the threshold, only craning your neck to see me in bed and out of consideration only waving to me with your hand. At times like that one would lie back and weep for happiness, and one weeps again now writing about it.

You also possess an especially beautiful, seldom-seen kind of quiet, contented and approving smile, which can make the person for whom it is meant entirely happy. I cannot remember that it was ever granted me specifically during my childhood, but it may well have been, for why should you have denied it to me at a time when I still seemed blameless to you and was your great hope. By the way, even such friendly impressions did not achieve anything more in the long run than to magnify my sense of guilt and make the world even more incomprehensible to me.

I would rather keep to the factual and constant. To assert myself even a little against you, and partly also out of a kind of vengefulness, I soon began to observe, collect and exaggerate ridiculous little things that I noticed about you. For example, the way you easily let yourself be dazzled by people only seemingly above you and how you could keep talking about them, as of some Imperial Councillor or the like (on the other hand, things like that also pained me, that you, my father, needed to believe such trifling confirmations of your own worth, and boasted about them). Or I would observe your predilection for indecent expressions, uttering them as loudly as possible, and laughing about them as though you had said something particularly splendid, while in fact it was merely a dull, petty impropriety (at the same time, however, for me it was another humiliating expression of your vitality). There were, of course, many different observations of this kind; I was happy about them, they gave me a reason for whispering and joking, you sometimes noticed it, got angry about it, considered it malice and lack of respect, but believe me, it was nothing more to me than a means – a useless one, moreover – of self-preservation, they were jokes of the kind one makes about gods and kings, jokes which are not only bound to the deepest respect, but even belong to it.

You too, by the way, in keeping with your similar situation regarding me, tried a kind of resistance. You used to point out how exaggeratedly well-off I was and how well I had in fact been treated. That is right, but I don't believe that it was of any fundamental use to me under the prevailing circumstances.

It is true that Mother was infinitely good to me, but for me all that stood in relation to you, therefore not in a good relation. Mother unconsciously played the role of the beater in a hunt. Even if in some unlikely event your upbringing could somehow have set me on my own feet by producing spite, aversion or even hatred in me, Mother balanced it out again by her kindness, her sensible talk (she was, in the chaos of childhood, the prototype of good sense), by interceding for me, and I was again driven back into your orbit, from which I might otherwise have broken free, to both your and my advantage. Or it was the case that no real reconciliation came about, that Mother merely protected me from you secretly, secretly gave me something, allowed me something, then before you I was once again that furtive creature, the cheat, the one with a guilty conscience, who because of his worthlessness could only surreptitiously get what he considered as his due. Of course, I then got used to looking by such means for those things which, even in my opinion, I wasn't entitled to. This again meant an increase in my sense of guilt.

It is also true that you hardly ever actually beat me. But that shouting, the way you turned red in the face, the hasty undoing of your suspenders, laying them ready over the back of the chair, was almost worse for me. It is as though someone is going to be hanged. If he really is hanged, then he is dead and it is all over. But if he has to go through all the preparations for his hanging and learns of his pardon only when the noose is hanging before his face, then he may suffer from this for the rest of his life. Moreover, from all of the many times when I had, in your clearly stated opinion, deserved a thrashing but was spared at the last moment by your grace, I again only accumulated a great sense of guilt. I was indebted to you on all fronts.

You always reproached me (and me alone or in front of others, you had no feeling for the humiliating effect of the latter, whatever concerned your children was always public) for living, thanks to your hard work, in peace and quiet, warmth and abundance, deprived of nothing. Then I think of your remarks which positively must have drawn furrows in my brain, such as: "When I was only seven I had to push the wheelbarrow from village to village." "We all had to sleep in one room." "We were glad when we had potatoes." "For years I had open sores on my legs because of inadequate winter clothing." "When I was only a little boy I was sent to Pisek to work in a store." "I got nothing from home, not even in the army, even then I was sending money home." "But for all that, for all that, Father was always Father to me. Who knows what that means today? What do the children know? No one's been through that! Does any child understand such things today?" Under other circumstances, such stories might have been very educational; they might have provided encouragement and strength to survive similar trials and deprivations as one's father had endured. But, of course, that was not what you wanted at all, the situation had, after all, become a different one through your efforts, there was no opportunity to distinguish oneself as you had done. One would first have had to create such an opportunity through violence and subversion, one would have had to break away from home (provided one had the decisiveness and strength to do it, and Mother, for her part, did not work against it with other means). But, of course, that was not what you wanted at all, you called this ingratitude, overexcitedness, disobedience, betrayal, madness. So, while on the one hand you tempted me to it with example, story and shame, on the other hand you strictly prohibited it with the utmost severity. Otherwise, for example, you would actually have had to be delighted by Ottla's Zürau adventure, apart from the accompanying circumstances.[14] She wanted to go to the country, from which you had come, she wanted work and hardship as you'd had, she did not want to enjoy the fruits of your hard work just as you yourself had been independent of your father. Were these such terrible intentions? So remote from your example and your teaching? All right, in the end Ottla's intentions failed in practice, they were perhaps carried out in a somewhat ridiculous way, with too much fuss, and she didn't have enough consideration for her parents. But was that exclusively her fault, not also the fault of the circumstances and especially the fact that you were so estranged from her? Was she any less estranged

---

[14] Ottla was dissatisfied with her job as assistant in her father's shop and instead applied for a place in an agricultural school in 1917. In the same year she took over the management of a farm in the northwest Bohemian town of Zürau. The farm belonged to her brother-in-law, Karl Hermann, who had been conscripted into the military. Her parents showed no understanding for her decision.

from you (as you later tried to convince yourself) in the shop than afterwards in Zürau? And wouldn't you certainly have had the power (provided you could have brought yourself to do so) to make something good come out of this adventure by means of encouragement, advice and supervision, perhaps even only by means of toleration?

After such experiences you used to say, joking bitterly, that we were too well off. But this joke is, in a certain sense, no joke at all. What you'd had to fight for we received from your hand; but the fight for external life, a fight that was instantly accessible to you and which we are, of course, not spared either, we have to fight later, as adults with the strength of a child. I'm not saying that our situation is therefore necessarily less advantageous than yours was, it is more likely equivalent (this is said, however, without comparing our basic characters), we are only at a disadvantage in that we are not able to boast of our poverty or humiliate anyone with it as you did with your poverty. And I don't deny that it might have been possible for me to really enjoy and appreciate the fruits of your great and successful work, and that I could have continued to work with them to your joy, but our estrangement stood in the way. I could enjoy whatever you gave, but only in shame, weariness, weakness, with a guilty conscience. That's why I could show my thanks to you for everything only as a beggar does, and not by deeds.

The next external consequence of this whole upbringing was that I fled everything that even remotely reminded me of you. First the shop. Actually, especially in my childhood, as long as it was still a small, simple shop, I ought to have liked it very much, it was so lively, lit up in the evening there was so much to see and to hear, one could help here and there, and distinguish oneself, but above all admire you with your magnificent commercial talents, how you sold things, dealt with people, joked, were untiring, in cases of doubt at once knew the right decision, and so on; even the way you wrapped a parcel or unpacked a crate was a sight worth seeing, the whole of it all in all not the worst schooling for a child. But since you gradually began to terrify me on all sides, and the shop and you became inseparable for me, the shop was no longer a comfortable place for me to be. Things which had at first been a matter of course for me began to torment and shame me, especially your treatment of the staff. I don't know, perhaps this was the case in most shops (at Assecuracioni Generali, for example, in my time it was really similar, I explained my resignation to the director there, not quite truthfully but not entirely a lie either, by the fact that I could not stand the cursing, which, incidentally, had not even been meant for me directly; I was too painfully sensitive to this from home), but the other shops did not concern me during my childhood. But you I heard and saw screaming, cursing and raging in the shop, in a manner that, in my opinion at the time, had no equal anywhere in the world. And not only abuse, but other tyrannies, too. For example, the way you jerked goods down off the counter that you did not want to have mixed up with the other things – only the blindness of your rage excused you a little – and how the sales clerk had to pick them up. Or your constant comments about a sales clerk suffering from tuberculosis: "Let him croak, the sick dog." You called your employees "paid enemies," and this they were, but even before they became that, you seemed to me to be their "paying enemy." There, too, I learned the great lesson that you could be unjust; in my case I would not have noticed it so soon for I had accumulated too many feelings of guilt, which made me ready to agree with you; but in my childish opinion – later, of course, somewhat modified, although not all too much so – there were strangers in the shop who nevertheless worked for us, and because of this had to live in perpetual fear of you. Of course I exaggerated, because I simply assumed that you had just as terrible an effect on those people as on me. If that had been the case, they could not have been able to live at all; but since they were adults with mostly excellent nerves, they effortlessly shook off your abuse and in the end it did you much more harm than it did them. For me, however, it made the shop intolerable, it reminded me far too much of my relationship to you: you were, quite apart from your entrepreneurial interest and apart from your need to be domineering, even as a businessman so greatly superior to all those who ever trained with you that none of their accomplishments could ever satisfy you, and you must similarly have been forever dissatisfied with me, too. That's why I necessarily took the side of the staff, incidentally also because I could not, out of anxiety, comprehend how anyone could be so abusive to a stranger, and that is why, out of anxiety, I somehow tried to reconcile the, in my opinion, very angry staff with you, with our family, if only for the sake of my own security. To this end it was not sufficient to behave in an ordinary, decent manner toward the staff, not even more modestly, it was more the case that I had to be humble, not only be the first to give a greeting but, if at all possible, to deflect any return greeting, too. And even if I, the insignificant person, had licked their feet downstairs, it would still have been no compensation for the way you, the Master, would hack at them upstairs. This relationship that I developed to my fellow man influenced me beyond the shop and into the future (something similar, but not as dangerous and far-reaching as in my case is, for example, Ottla's predilection for associating with poor people, sitting together with the servant girls, and similar behaviour, which annoys you so much). In the end I was almost afraid of the shop, and in any case it had long ceased to be a concern of mine even before I reached secondary school and was taken even further away from it. It also seemed very much beyond my capabilities since, as you said, it exhausted even yours. You then tried (today this is both touching and humiliating for me) nevertheless to draw a little sweetness for yourself from my aversion to the shop and your work – an aversion which was, after all, very painful for you – by claiming that I lacked business sense, that I had loftier ideas in my head, and the like. Mother was, of course, delighted with this explanation, which you squeezed out of yourself, and I too, in my vanity and need, let myself be influenced by it. But had it really only, or primarily, been "loftier ideas" which turned me away from the shop (which I now, but only now, really and honestly hate), they would have had to express themselves differently than letting me swim quietly and anxiously through secondary school and my law studies until I finally landed at a clerk's desk.

If I had wanted to escape from you, I would have had to escape from the family, too, even from Mother. One could always get protection from her, true enough, but only in relation to you. She loved you too much and was much too loyal and devoted to you to have been an independent spiritual force in the child's struggle for any length of time. A correct instinct on the part of the child, by the way, for over the years Mother became ever more closely allied to you; while, in whatever concerned her, she always preserved her independence, beautifully and delicately within the narrowest limits and without ever essentially hurting you; more and more over the years she nevertheless, emotionally rather than intellectually, blindly accepted your judgements and condemnations with regard to the children, particularly in the case – a difficult one, it is true – of Ottla. Of course, one always has to keep in mind how agonizing and utterly wearing Mother's position in the family was. She toiled in the shop and at home, suffered doubly all the family illnesses, but the culmination of all this was what she suffered in her intermediate position between us and you. You were always loving and considerate toward her, but in this regard you spared her just as little as we did. We hammered at her ruthlessly, you from your side, we from ours. It was a distraction, one didn't mean any harm, one thought only of the battle which you were waging with us and we with you, and it was on Mother that we took out our feelings. Nor was it a good contribution to child-rearing how you – without any fault on your part, of course – tormented her because of us. It even seemed to justify our otherwise unjustifiable behaviour toward her. How she suffered from us because of you and from you because of us, not even including those cases in which you were in the right, because she spoiled us, even if this "spoiling" may sometimes have only been a quiet, unconscious counter-demonstration against your system. Of course, Mother would not have been able to endure all of this if she hadn't drawn the strength to endure it from the love she had for all of us and her happiness in this love.

My sisters were only partly with me. Happiest in her relation to you was Valli. Being closest to Mother, she obeyed you in a similar way, without much effort or suffering too much harm. But you accepted her also in a friendlier way, simply because she reminded you of Mother, despite there being little of the Kafka material in her. But perhaps this was precisely what you wanted; where there was nothing of the Kafka element, not even you could ask for anything of the sort; nor did you have the feeling, as did the rest of us, that something was getting lost here which had to be saved by force. Besides, you may never really have liked the Kafka element as it expressed itself in women. Valli's relationship to you might perhaps have become even friendlier if we others hadn't interfered with it somewhat.

Elli is the only example of someone almost completely successful in breaking out of your orbit. I expected it of her the least when she was a child. She was such a clumsy, tired, timid, morose, guilt-ridden, overly humble, malicious, lazy, greedy, stingy child I could hardly look at her, certainly not speak to her, so much did she remind me of myself, so very similarly was she under the same spell of our upbringing. Her miserliness was especially repulsive to me, since I had it to an, if possible, even greater degree. Miserliness is, after all, one of the most reliable symptoms of deep unhappiness; I was so uncertain of everything that I really only possessed what I already held in my hands or had in my mouth, or what was at least on the way there, and this was precisely what she, who was in a similar situation, enjoyed taking away from me. But this all changed when at a young age – this is the main thing – she left home, married, had children, became cheerful, carefree, brave, generous, unselfish, hopeful. It is almost unbelievable that you didn't really notice this change at all, or in any case did not give it its due, blinded as you were by the grudge you have always had against Elli and still have, fundamentally unchanged, today; only this grudge has become much less relevant now since Elli no longer lives with us, and besides, your love for Felix and your fondness for Karl have made it less important. Only Gerti must sometimes still pay for it.

About Ottla I hardly dare to write; I know that by doing so I'm jeopardizing the entire hoped-for effect of this letter. Under normal circumstances, that is, if she is not in any particular need or danger, you feel only hatred for her; you even admitted to me that, in your opinion, she intentionally causes you constant suffering and annoyance, and while you are suffering because of her she is satisfied and content. A kind of devil, then. What a colossal estrangement, even greater than that between you and me, must have developed to make possible such a dreadful misjudgement. She is so remote from you that you hardly see her anymore, instead you put a phantom in the place where you suppose her to be. I admit that you had a particularly difficult time with her. Of course, I don't quite see through this very complicated case, but at any rate here was something of a kind of Löwy equipped with the best Kafka weapons. Between us there was no real struggle; I was soon finished off; what remained was flight, bitterness, sorrow, inner struggle. But you two are always on guard, always fresh, always energetic. A sight as magnificent as it was miserable. At the very first you were, I am sure, very close to one another, for even today Ottla is, of the four of us, perhaps the purest representation of the marriage between you and Mother and of the forces it combined. I don't know what deprived you of the happiness of the harmony between father and child, but I am tempted to believe that the development was similar to mine. On your side was the tyranny of your nature, on her side the

Löwy defiance, sensitivity, sense of justice, restlessness, and all of it supported by an awareness of the Kafka energy. Doubtless I too influenced her, but hardly of my own doing, rather by the mere fact of my existence. Besides, as the last to enter into the already established balance of power, she was able to form her own judgement from the large amount of material available to her. I can even imagine that for some time, in her innermost being, she wavered between throwing herself at your breast or that of the adversaries, obviously you failed to do something at that time and repelled her, but if it had at all been possible, you would have made a splendidly harmonious pair. True, I would have lost an ally as a result, but the sight of you two would have richly compensated me, and the immeasurable happiness of finding complete contentment in at least one child would have transformed you very much to my benefit. Today, however, this is all just a dream. Ottla has no contact with her father, has to find her way alone, like me, and the greater amount of trust, self-confidence, health and decisiveness that she has compared to me makes her in your eyes more wicked and treacherous than me. I understand that; from your point of view she cannot be any different. Indeed, she herself is capable of seeing herself through your eyes, sharing your suffering and being – not despairing, despair is my business – very sad. You do see us together often, in apparent contradiction to this, whispering and laughing, now and then you hear your name mentioned, you get the impression of impudent conspirators. Strange conspirators. Admittedly, you have been a main topic of our conversations, as of our thoughts, ever since we can remember, but we truly do not sit together to plot against you, but rather to discuss with all our might, in fun, in seriousness, in love, defiance, rage, disgust, surrender, feelings of guilt, with all the strength of our heads and hearts, this terrible trial which hangs between us and you, in all its details, from all sides, on all occasions, from far and near, this trial in which you incessantly claim to be the judge, while you are, at least mostly (here I leave a wide margin for all the errors which I may, of course, make) just as weak and deluded a party to it as we are.

An example of the effect of your upbringing, very instructive in the context of the whole situation, was Irma[15]. On the one hand she was, after all, a stranger who entered your business already an adult and dealt with you mainly as her boss, was thus only partly, and at an age when she already had powers of resistance, exposed to your influence; but on the other hand she was also a blood relative, honoured you as the brother of her father, and you had much more power over her than that of a mere boss. And even so she – who was with her frail body so efficient, clever, hard-working, modest, trustworthy, unselfish and loyal, who loved you as her uncle and admired you as her boss, she who proved herself in previous and subsequent positions – was not a very good clerk to you. In relation to you she was close to being one of your own children – pushed by us too, of course – and so great was the power of your personality to bend others, in her case, too, that (admittedly only in relation to you and, hopefully, without the deeper suffering of a child) she developed forgetfulness, carelessness, a sardonic humor, perhaps even a little spite, as far as she was capable of that at all, and I don't even take into account that she was ailing or otherwise quite unhappy

[15] Irma Kafka (1889–1919), the daughter of Franz's Uncle Ludwig, who died in 1911, was employed in Hermann Kafka's shop. She befriended Ottla and, like her, could only with difficulty fit into the business.

and that she was burdened with a dreary home life. What was for me so rich in associations in your relation to her you yourself summed up in a sentence that has become a classic for us, one that was almost blasphemous but extremely telling precisely because of your innocence about your treatment of people: "The blessed one has left me quite a mess."

I could describe other spheres of your influence and the struggle against it, but here I would enter uncertain territory and would have to fabricate; besides, the more you distance yourself from business and family, the friendlier, more accommodating, polite, considerate, sympathetic (I mean outwardly, too) you become, just as, for example, an autocrat does when one day he happens to be outside the borders of his own country, has no reason to go on being tyrannical and can associate good-naturedly even with the most common people. Indeed, in the group photos from Franzensbad, for example, you always looked as big and cheerful among the sullen, little people as a king on his travels. As a matter of fact, this was something that could have been an advantage to the children, too, only they would have had to be able to recognize it already as children, which was impossible, and I, for example, would not have had to live constantly in the innermost, strictest, binding circle of your influence as, in fact, I did.

I lost not only, as you say, my sense of family because of this; on the contrary, I still had a sense of family, albeit mainly a negative one, concerned with my emancipation from you (which, of course, was never to be achieved). But relations with people outside the family suffered possibly even more under your influence. You are completely mistaken if you think I do everything for other people out of love and loyalty and, out of coldness and treachery, nothing for you and the family. I repeat for the tenth time: I would probably have become a shy and anxious person in any case, but it is still a long, dark road from there to where I have really come. (Until now I have intentionally concealed relatively little in this letter, but now and later I am going to have to keep silent about some things that are still too difficult for me to admit to you and to myself. I am saying this so that if the overall picture should here and there become somewhat blurred, you won't believe it is for lack of evidence; there is much more evidence available that could make the picture unbearably harsh. It is not easy to find a middle way). Here, in any case, it suffices to remember something from the early days: I had lost my self-confidence where you were concerned, had traded it for a boundless sense of guilt. (In recollection of this boundlessness I once wrote of someone, accurately, "He is afraid the shame will outlive him.") I couldn't suddenly transform myself whenever I was with other people; rather, I developed an even deeper sense of guilt in relation to them for, as I've already said, I had to make up to them the wrongs you had done them in the shop, wrongs which I too shared responsibility for. Besides, you had some objection to make, openly or secretly, about everyone I associated with, and for this too I had to offer them my apologies. The distrust that you tried to instill in me toward most people at the shop and at home (name me one person who was somehow of importance to me in my childhood whom you didn't criticize to the ground at least once) did not, strangely enough, burden you particularly (you were simply strong enough to endure it, besides it was perhaps really only an emblem of the ruler); this distrust, which was nowhere confirmed in my own eyes as a little boy, since I saw everywhere only people of unattainable excellence, became in me distrust of myself and a perpetual fear of everyone else. There I was certainly not able to save myself from you. That you were mistaken about this is perhaps because you didn't actually learn anything about my dealings with other people, and you suspiciously and jealously assumed (do I deny that you love me?) that I had to compensate for the lack of a family life in another way, since it must be impossible for me to live away from home in the same way. By the way, in this respect I still had in my childhood a certain comfort in my very distrust of my own judgement; I would say to myself: "Come on, you're exaggerating; you feel, as young people always do, trivialities too much as great exceptions." But I later almost lost this comfort as my perspective of the world became clearer.

I found just as little deliverance from you in Judaism. Here, deliverance would have been conceivable, in principle, but what is more, it would have been conceivable for us to find one another in Judaism or we might even have started out from there in harmony. But what kind of Judaism was it that I got from you! I have, over the course of time, taken more or less three attitudes to it.

As a child, in agreement with you, I blamed myself for not going often enough to the synagogue, for not fasting, and so on. I believed that in this way I was wronging you, not me, and guilt feelings, always at the ready, ran through me.

Later, as a young adult, I could not understand how you, with the trifle of Judaism which you possessed, could accuse me (out of piety, really, as you expressed it) of not making the effort to cling to a similar trifle. It was really, as far as I could tell, a mere trifle, a joke, not even a joke. You went to the temple four days a year, where

you were, to say the least, closer at least to the indifferent than to those who took it seriously, patiently went through the prayers as a formality, sometimes amazed me by being able to show me in the prayer book the passage that was just being recited, and other than that, so long as I was (and this was the main thing) present in the synagogue I was allowed to hang around wherever I wanted. So I yawned and dozed away the many hours there (I don't think I was ever so bored again until dancing lessons) and tried as best I could to enjoy the few small diversions there were, for instance, when the Ark of the Covenant was opened, which always reminded me of the shooting galleries where a cupboard door would open whenever you hit a bull's eye, only there something interesting always came out, and here it was always the same old dolls without heads.[16] Incidentally, I was also very frightened there, not only, of course, because of all the people one came in contact with, but also because you once mentioned in passing that I too might be called to the Torah.[17] That was something I dreaded for years. But other than that I was not fundamentally disturbed in my boredom, perhaps by the bar mitzvah[18], but that only required some ridiculous rote learning, in other words, it led only to a ridiculous passing of an exam, and then, what concerns you, by small, not very significant incidents, like when you were called to the Torah and did well in what felt to me purely a social event, or when you remained in the temple for the prayers for the dead and I would be sent away, which,

---

[16] Here are meant the scrolls rolled in their cloth covers.
[17] Chosen members of the congregation can be called up for the reading of the Torah.
[18] This ceremony grants male youths religious maturity upon completion of their thirteenth year.

for a long time – apparently because of having been sent away, and the lack of any deeper interest – gave rise in me to a feeling I was hardly aware of, that something indecent was going on. That's how it was in the synagogue; at home it was, if possible, even shabbier and limited to the first Seder[19], which developed increasingly into a farce with fits of laughter, admittedly under the influence of the maturing children. (Why did you have to give way to this influence? Because you brought it about.) This, then, was the religious material that was handed down to me, added to this was at most the outstretched hand pointing to "the sons of the millionaire Fuchs," who on the high holy days came to the synagogue with their father.[20] I did not understand how to do anything better with this material than get rid of it as quickly as possible; precisely this ridding myself of it seemed to me the most pious act.

Later still I perceived it differently again and understood why it was possible for you to believe that in this respect, too, I was maliciously betraying you. You really had brought some traces of Judaism with you from the small ghetto-like village community, it was not much and faded a little more in the city and during your military service, even so the impressions and memories of your youth did just suffice for some sort of Jewish life, especially since you didn't need much help of that kind, but rather came of robust stock and your personality could scarcely be shaken by religious scruples unless they were strongly mixed with social scruples. In principle, the most prominent belief in your life consisted in your

---

[19] This celebration takes place in the household on the first two evenings of Passover.
[20] Here Kafka is criticizing his father's tendency to regard worship service primarily as a business meeting place.

believing in the unconditional correctness of the opinions of a certain class of Jewish society and actually, since these opinions belonged to your own nature, that you believed yourself. Even in this there was still enough Judaism, but it was too little to be passed on to the child, it dribbled away entirely while you were passing it on. In part it was impressions of youth that could not be passed on, in part it was your dreaded personality. It was also impossible to make clear to a child who from sheer anxiety was too acutely observant that those few trivialities you performed in the name of Judaism, with an indifference corresponding to their triviality, could have any higher meaning. For you they were meaningful as small souvenirs of earlier times and that's why you wanted to impart them to me, but you could do so only by way of persuasion or threat, since they no longer had any value of their own, even for you; on the one hand this could not succeed, and on the other hand, since you did not recognize your weak position here, it had to make you very angry with me because of my apparent obstinacy.

The whole thing is, of course, no isolated phenomenon, it was much the same with a large portion of this transitional generation of Jews which migrated from the comparatively still pious countryside to the cities; it happened of itself, but it added to our relationship, which was certainly not lacking in fierceness, one more sufficiently painful source of bitterness. In that regard you should in this point also believe in your guiltlessness, just as I do, but explain this guiltlessness by your nature and by the circumstances of the time, and not merely by external circumstances, that is, not merely say, for instance, that you had too much other work and worries to be able to bother with such things as well. This is how you often turn your undisputed guiltlessness into an unjust reproach of others. That is then very easy to refute, everywhere and here too. It would not have been a question of any sort of instruction you should have given your children, but of an exemplary life; had your Judaism been stronger, then your example would also have been more compelling, that is obvious and again is not at all a reproach but merely a rejection of your reproaches. You've recently been reading Franklin's memoirs of his youth. I really did purposely give it to you to read, but not, as you ironically remarked, because of a small passage on vegetarianism[21], but because of the relationship between the author and his father as it is there described, and of the relationship between the author and his son, how it is spontaneously expressed in these memoirs written for the son. I don't want to go into details here.

I have received a certain retrospective confirmation of this view of your Judaism from your conduct in recent years, when it seemed to you that I was taking more of an interest in Jewish matters. Since from the outset you have had an aversion to all of my activities and especially to the nature of my interest, so you had it here, too. But in spite of this, one could have expected you to make a small exception here. It was, after all, Judaism of your Judaism that was here stirring, and with it also the possibility of establishing a new relationship between us. I do not deny that if you'd shown interest in them, these things might have become suspect to me for that very reason. It doesn't occur to me in the least to want to claim that I am in this regard any better than you. But it never came to the test. Because of my connection with

---

[21] Kafka decided on a meatless diet early on, thus provoking his father and, in this regard too, taking on the role of an outsider within the family.

it, Judaism became repulsive to you, Jewish writings unreadable, they "nauseated you." This might have meant that you insisted that only that Judaism you had shown me in my childhood was the right one, beyond that there was nothing. Yet that you should insist on this was really scarcely conceivable. But then the "nausea" (aside from the fact that it was directed primarily not against Judaism but against my person) could only mean that you unconsciously acknowledged the weakness of your Judaism and my Jewish upbringing, in no way wanted to be reminded of this and reacted to any reminder with open hatred. By the way, your negative high esteem for my new Judaism was very exaggerated; in the first place it bore your curse within it and, second, for its development the fundamental relationship to one's fellow man was decisive, and therefore fatal, in my case.

You struck closer to home with your aversion to my writing and what, unknown to you, was connected with it. Here I actually got some distance from you independently, even if it brings to mind a little the worm that, having had a foot step on its tail end, tears its front part free and drags itself off to the side. To some extent I was in safety, there was a sigh of relief; the aversion that you naturally and immediately had to my writing was for once welcome to me. Although my vanity, my ambition, suffered under your now famous way of greeting the arrival of my books: "Put it on the night table!" (usually you were playing cards when a book arrived), this was actually quite all right with me, not only out of rebellious malice, not only out of delight at a new confirmation of my view of our relationship, but quite spontaneously, because that formula sounded to me something like "Now you are free!" Of course, it was a delusion, I was not – or, in the very best case, not yet – free. My writing was about you, all I did there was lament what I couldn't lament at your breast. It was an intentionally drawn-out farewell from you, and though it was really forced by you, it proceeded in the direction I determined. But how little all that was! It is only worth talking about at all because it occurred in my life, anywhere else it would not even be noted, and also because in my childhood it ruled my life as a presentiment, later as a hope, later still often as despair, and it dictated – if you will, once again in your shape – my few petty decisions.

For example, the choice of career. True, here you gave me complete freedom in your generous and, in this sense, even patient manner. Though here again you followed the general way of treating sons of the Jewish middle class, which was the standard for you, or at least the values of this class. Finally, one of your misunderstandings regarding my person played a part here, too. Out of paternal pride, ignorance of my real existence, conclusions drawn from my feebleness, you have always taken me to be particularly industrious. As a child I was, in your opinion, always studying and later always writing. That is not even remotely the case. One can sooner say, and with much less exaggeration, that I studied little and learned nothing. That after those many years something did stick in my mind thanks to a moderately good memory and a not too inferior intellect is, after all, not so remarkable, but in any case the overall result of knowledge, and especially the solid grounding of knowledge, is exceedingly deplorable in comparison to the expenditure of time and money amid an outwardly carefree, peaceful life, especially also in comparison to almost everyone I know. It is deplorable, but to me understandable. I have, ever since I was able to think, had such profound anxieties about asserting my spiritual existence that I was indifferent to everything else. Jewish high school students here are often odd, you find the most unlikely things among them, but my cold, hardly disguised, indestructible, childishly helpless to the point of being ridiculous, brutishly self-satisfied indifference, the indifference of a self-satisfied but coldly imaginative child, I have never found anywhere else; to be sure, it was here too the only protection against a nervous breakdown brought on by fear and a sense of guilt. All that occupied my mind was concern for myself, and this in various ways. There was, for instance, the concern about my health; it started easily enough, now and then there arose a little anxiety about my digestion, my loss of hair, a spinal curvature and so on, increasing in innumerable gradations, finally ending in a real illness. But since there was nothing at all I was certain of, since I needed a new confirmation of my existence at every instant, since nothing was in my very own indubitable sole possession, determined unambiguously only by me, in truth a disinherited son, naturally I became unsure of even the things nearest to me, my own body. I grew very tall but didn't know what to do with my height, the burden was too great, my back became bent; I hardly dared to move, let alone exercise, I remained weak; I regarded everything I still had at my command as a miracle, for instance, my good digestion; that sufficed to lose it, and with that the way was open to every form of hypochondria until finally, under the superhuman effort of wanting to marry (of this I shall speak later), blood came from the lung, something in which the apartment in the Schönborn palace – which, however, I needed only because I believed I needed it for my writing, so that this too belongs on this page – may have played a sufficient part. So all this did not originate in excessive work, as you always imagine. There were years during which, in the best of health, I whiled away more time on the sofa than you did in your entire life, all your illnesses included. When I rushed away from you terribly busy, it was usually to go lie down in my room. My total output of work done, both in the office (where, of course, laziness is not really conspicuous and moreover was kept in check by my timidity) and at home, is minute; if you had any idea of it, it would appall you. Probably I am constitutionally not lazy at all, but there was nothing for me to do. Where I lived I was rejected, condemned, subdued, and though to flee elsewhere was an enormous strain, it was not work, for it had to do with something impossible, something that was, with small exceptions, beyond my powers.

In this state, then, I was given the freedom to choose a career. But was I still capable of actually making any use at all of such freedom? Did I really still believe that I was capable of achieving a real career? My self-esteem was much more dependent on you than on anything else, such as external success. That was the consolation of a moment, nothing more, but on the other side your weight always pulled me down much more strongly. Never would I get through the first grade of elementary school, I thought, but I succeeded, and even received a prize; but I would certainly never pass the entrance exam for secondary school, but I succeeded; but now I'll definitely fail the first year of secondary school, no, I didn't fail and I succeeded again and again. This did not produce any confidence, however; on the contrary, I was always convinced – and I had positive proof of it in your cold expression – that the more I succeeded, the worse it would have to turn out. Often in my mind's eye I saw the terrible assembly of the teachers (secondary school is only the most coherent example, but everywhere around me it was similar) as they would meet when I'd passed the first class, and then in the second class, when I'd passed that, and then in the third and so on, in order to examine this unique, outrageous case, how I, the most incapable and, in any case, the most ignorant of all, had succeeded in creeping up so far as this class, which, now that everyone's attention was fixed on me, would of course instantly spew me out, to the jubilation of all the righteous, now liberated from this nightmare. To live with such fantasies is not easy for a child. What, under these circumstances, did I care about my lessons? Who was able to strike a spark of interest in me? The lessons interested me – and not only the lessons but everything around me at this crucial age – as with an embezzling bank clerk who, still at his job and trembling at the thought of being discovered, takes interest in the petty routine business of the bank that he still has to see to. That was how small, how remote everything was compared to the main thing. This continued up to the school-leaving exam, which I really got through partly by cheating, and then it slackened, now I was free. If, despite the pressure of secondary school, I had already been concerned only with myself, how much more now that I was free. So there was no real freedom in the choice of profession for me, I knew: in consideration of the main thing I would be just as indifferent to everything else as I had been to all the subjects at secondary school, so it was a matter of finding a profession that would most likely allow me to indulge this indifference without injuring my vanity all too much. Therefore, law was the obvious choice. Small, contrary attempts on the part of vanity, of senseless hope, such as a fourteen-day study of chemistry or a half-year of German studies, only strengthened that fundamental conviction. So I studied law. This meant that in the few months before the exams, in a way that severely tested my nerves, I literally nourished myself, intellectually speaking, on sawdust that had, moreover, already been chewed by a thousand mouths. But in a certain sense this was exactly to my taste, as in a certain sense the secondary school had been earlier and later my job as a clerk, for it all completely suited my situation. Anyway, I showed astonishing foresight here, even as a small child I had had fairly clear premonitions with regard to my studies and my profession. From here I wasn't expecting any rescue, I'd long ago given that up.

But I showed no foresight at all concerning the significance and possibility of a marriage for me; this, so far the greatest terror of my life, has come upon me almost completely unexpectedly. The child had developed so slowly, these things were outwardly all too remote from him; now and then the necessity of thinking about them did arise; but that here a perpetual, decisive and even most bitter ordeal was being prepared was impossible to recognize. In reality, however, the attempts at marriage became the most magnificent and hopeful rescue attempts, and correspondingly magnificent were their failure.

I'm afraid that as I fail at everything in this area, I will also fail in clarifying these attempts at marriage for you. And yet the success of this entire letter depends on it, for on the one hand everything that I had at my disposal in the way of positive forces was gathered into these attempts, and on the other hand here all the negative forces that I have described as the consequence of your child-rearing method – that is, the weakness, the lack of self-confidence, the sense of guilt – also accumulated, and with downright fury literally drew a cordon between me and marriage. The explanation will be difficult for me also because I have spent so many days and nights thinking and digging through everything that now the sight of it confuses even me. The only thing that makes the explanation easier for me is your, in my opinion, complete misunderstanding of the matter; to correct such a complete misunderstanding slightly does not seem too difficult.

First of all, you rank my failures at marriage with the rest of my failures; in principle, I wouldn't really have anything against this provided you accept my previous explanation of my failure. It is really part of the same series, only you underestimate the significance of the matter, and underestimate it so much that whenever we talk about it, we are actually talking about quite different things. I dare say that nothing has happened to you in your entire life that has had such significance for you as the attempts at marriage have had for me. I don't mean by this that you've not experienced anything in itself as significant; on the contrary, your life was much richer and full of worries and more packed than mine, but that is exactly why nothing of this sort has happened to you. It is as if one person had to climb five low steps and a second person only one, but one which is, at least for him, as high as those five put together; the first person will not only manage the five but hundreds and thousands as well, he will have led a great and very strenuous life, but none of the steps he has climbed will have had the significance for him as that one first, high step had for the second, which for all his strength was impossible to climb and which he cannot get up onto and which he naturally doesn't get past, either.

Marrying, founding a family, accepting all the children

that arrive, supporting them in this uncertain world and perhaps even guiding them a little is, I am convinced, the utmost a human being can succeed in doing at all. That so many seem to succeed at it so easily is no evidence to the contrary for, first of all, not many really succeed at it and, second, these not-many usually don't "do" it, it merely "happens" to them; this is not this utmost but it is still very great and very honourable (especially as "doing" and "happening" are not absolutely separable). And, finally, it is not even a matter of this utmost at all, but only of some distant but decent approximation; it is, after all, not necessary to fly right into the middle of the sun, but it is necessary to crawl to a clean little spot on earth where the sun sometime shines and one can warm oneself a little.

So how was I prepared for this? As badly as possible. That emerges from what has been said up to now. But as far as there is any direct preparation of the individual, and any direct creation of the general basic conditions exists, you didn't intervene much outwardly. It could not be any other way; decisive here are the general sexual customs of class, nation and time. All the same, you did intervene here too – not much, for the requirement of such intervention can only be strong mutual trust, and we were both lacking in this even long before the crucial time, and not very happily, as our needs were quite different; what seizes me hardly has to touch you at all and vice versa, what is innocence for you may be guilt for me and vice versa, what has no consequences for you may be the last nail in my coffin.

I remember going for a walk one evening with you and Mother, it was in Joseph's Square near where the Länderbank is today, and I began talking about these interesting things in a stupid, boastful, superior, proud, aloof (that was untrue), cold (that was true) and stuttering manner, as indeed I usually talked to you, reproaching the two of you for having left me uninstructed, with the fact that my classmates had to take me in hand, that I had been close to great dangers (here I was outrageously lying, as was my way, in order to appear brave, for as a consequence of my timidity I had no precise idea of these "great dangers"), but in the end hinted that now, luckily, I knew everything, no longer needed any advice, and that everything was fine. I had begun talking about this mainly because it gave me pleasure at least to talk about it, then also out of curiosity and finally to somehow avenge myself on you both for something or other. In keeping with your nature, you took it quite easily, you said only something to the effect that you could give me advice on how I could pursue these things without danger. Perhaps I'd wanted to entice just such an answer out of you, it was in keeping with the prurience of the child overfed with meat and all good things, physically inactive, eternally preoccupied with himself, but even so my outward sense of shame was so hurt by this, or I thought it ought to be so hurt, that against my will I couldn't speak to you any longer about this and with arrogant impudence broke off the conversation.

It is not easy to judge the answer you gave me then, on the one hand there is indeed something staggeringly open, somewhat primeval in it, on the other hand, though, it is as far as the lesson is concerned uninhibited in a very modern way. I don't remember how old I was at the time, I couldn't have been much older than sixteen. But for such a boy it was nevertheless a very curious answer and the distance between the two of us is also apparent in the fact that it was actually the first direct lesson about life that I received from you. Its real meaning, however, which already sank into me then but which came partly to the surface of my consciousness only much later, was the following: What you advised me to do was, in your opinion and even more in my opinion at the time, the filthiest thing imaginable. That you wanted to make sure that I didn't physically bring any of the filth home was beside the point, for you were only protecting yourself, your house. The main thing was much more that you remained outside your own advice, a married man, a pure man, superior to such things; this was probably intensified for me at the time by the fact that even marriage seemed to me shameless and it was therefore impossible for me to apply the general information I'd gleaned about marriage to my parents. In this way you became purer still, rose still higher. The thought that you could have given yourself a similar piece of advice before your marriage was to me utterly unthinkable. So there was hardly any smudge of earthly filth on you. And it was you who pushed me with a few frank words, as though I were predetermined to it, down into this filth. If the world therefore consisted of only me and you, an idea that I was much inclined to have, then this purity of the world ended with you and, by virtue of your advice, the filth began with me. In itself it was, of course, incomprehensible that you thus condemned me, it could only be explained to me by old guilt and the deepest contempt on your part. And so I was again seized by this in my innermost being, and very hard indeed.

Perhaps here both our guiltlessness becomes clearest. A gives B a piece of advice that is frank, in keeping with his attitude to life, not very nice but still even today perfectly usual in the city, a piece of advice that might prevent damage to health. This piece of advice is for B morally not very fortifying, but why shouldn't he be able to work his way out of the damage in the course of the years, in any case he doesn't even have to take the advice, and anyway there is no reason for the advice itself to cause B's entire future world to collapse around him. And yet, something of this kind does occur, but only because A is you and B is me.

I am able to see this mutual guiltlessness especially well because a similar clash between us occurred some twenty years later under completely different circumstances, terrible in itself, but in actual fact much less damaging, for where was something in me, a thirty-six-year-old, that could still be damaged? I'm referring here to a brief discussion on one of those few tumultuous days following the announcement of my latest plans to marry.[22] You said to me something like this: "She probably put on some well-chosen blouse, as Prague Jewish women are so good at, and right away, of course, you decided to marry her. And that as quickly as possible, in a week, tomorrow, today. I don't understand you, you're a grown man, after all, you live in the city and don't know any better than to marry the next best girl. Are there no other possibilities? If you are frightened of it, I'll go there with you myself." You spoke in greater detail and more plainly, but I can no longer remember the details, perhaps it also grew a little vague before my eyes, I paid almost more attention to Mother who, though in complete agreement with you, nevertheless took something from the table and left the room with it. You have hardly ever humiliated me more deeply with words or ever shown me your contempt more clearly. When you spoke to me similarly twenty years ago, one might, look-

---

[22] Kafka is alluding to his engagement to Julie Wohryzek (see note 8).

ing at it with your eyes, have seen some respect for the precocious city boy who, in your opinion, could already be initiated into life without further ado. Today, this consideration could only increase the contempt, for the boy who at that time was about to make a start got stuck and today seems to you not to have grown any richer in experience, only twenty years more pitiable. My choice of a girl meant nothing at all to you. You had (unconsciously) always suppressed my power of decision and now believed (unconsciously) you knew what it was worth. Of my attempts at escape in other directions you knew nothing, therefore you couldn't know anything either about the thought processes that led me to this attempt to marry, and had to try to guess at them, and in keeping with your general opinion of me you guessed at the most repulsive, crude and ridiculous alternative. And you didn't hesitate for a moment to tell me this in just such a manner. The shame that you inflicted on me with this was nothing to you compared to the shame that I would in your opinion inflict on your name by this marriage.

Now, regarding my attempts at marriage, there is much you can respond with, and you have done it, too: you could not have much respect for my decision since I'd twice broken my engagement to F.[23] and twice renewed it, since I'd needlessly dragged you and Mother to the engagement party in Berlin and the like. All of that is true, but how did it come to this?

The fundamental thought behind both marriage attempts was quite sound: to set up house, to become independent. An idea that appeals to you, except that in reality it turns out like the children's game in which one

---

[23] Felice Bauer (see note 8).

holds and even presses the other's hand while at the same time calling out, "Oh, go away, go away, why don't you go away?" Which in our case happens to be complicated by the fact that you have always honestly meant "Go away," but you have always, without knowing it, held me back, or, better, held me down merely by the force of your personality.

Although both girls were chosen by chance, they were extraordinarily well chosen. Yet another sign of your complete misunderstanding that you can think that I, timid, hesitant, suspicious, can decide to marry in a flash out of delight over a blouse. Both marriages would rather have been common-sense marriages, as long as it is thereby said that day and night, the first time for years, the second time for months, all my powers of thought were concentrated on the plan.

Neither of the girls disappointed me, only I disappointed both of them. My opinion of them today is exactly the same as when I wanted to marry them.

It is not true either that in my second marriage attempt I disregarded the experiences of the first, in other words that I was rash. The cases were simply quite different, precisely the earlier experience gave me hope for the second case, which was altogether much more promising. But I don't want to discuss details here.

Why, then, did I not marry? There were individual obstacles, as there are everywhere, but life consists in taking such obstacles. The essential obstacle, however, which is unfortunately independent of the individual case, was that obviously I am spiritually incapable of marrying. This is expressed in the fact that from the moment I decide to marry I can no longer sleep, my head burns day and night, it is no longer life, I stagger about in despair. It's not actual worries that cause this – true, in keeping with my ponderousness and pedantry, countless worries are involved in this, but they are not the deciding factor; like worms they complete the work on the corpse – but the decisive blow comes from elsewhere. It is the general pressure of anxiety, weakness, self-contempt.

I'll try to explain it in more detail: In the attempt to marry, two seemingly antagonistic elements in my relations with you combine more intensely than anywhere else. Marriage is certainly the pledge of the most acute form of self-liberation and independence. I'd have a family, in my opinion the highest one can achieve, so too the highest you have achieved, I'd be your equal, every old and eternally new shame and tyranny would be mere history. It would indeed be like a fairy tale, but precisely therein lies the questionable element. It's too much, so much can't be achieved. It is as though a person were captive and had not only the intention to escape, which might perhaps be attainable, but also, and at the same time, the intention to rebuild the prison into a pleasure dome for himself. But if he escapes he cannot rebuild and if he rebuilds he cannot escape. If I, in the particular unhappy relationship in which I stand to you, want to become independent, I'd have to do something that had, if at all possible, no connection to you in any way; though marrying is the greatest thing and provides the most honourable independence, it is also at the same time most closely connected to you. To try to get out of this has a certain madness in it, and each attempt is almost punished with it.

It is precisely this close connection that partly tempts me to marry. I envision this equality that would then arise between us, and which you would understand better than anyone else, as so beautiful because then I could be a free, grateful, guiltless, upright son, and you an untroubled, untyrannical, sympathetic, satisfied father. But for this purpose everything that ever happened would have to be undone, that means we ourselves would have to be obliterated. But being as we are, marrying is barred to me because it is your very own territory. Sometimes I imagine the map of the world spread out and you stretched diagonally across it. And then it seems to me as though I could consider living only in those places that you either do not cover or that do not lie within your reach. And, in keeping with the conception that I have of your size, these are not many and not very comforting regions, and especially marriage is not among them.

This comparison already proves that I in no way mean to say that you drove me away from marriage by your example as you'd driven me from your business. The opposite is true, despite every remote similarity. In your marriage I had what was, in many ways, a model marriage before me: model in devotedness, mutual help, number of children, and even when the children grew up and disturbed the peace all the more, the marriage as such remained undisturbed. Perhaps my lofty idea of marriage was formed precisely on this model; that the desire for marriage was powerless was due simply to other reasons. These lay in your relationship to your children, which is, after all, what this whole letter is about.

There is a view according to which fear of marriage sometimes stems from the fear that one's children would some day pay one back for the sins committed against one's own parents. This, I believe, is not of great significance in my case, for my sense of guilt actually stems from you, and is imbued with its uniqueness, indeed, this feeling of uniqueness is an essential part of its tormenting nature, any repetition is unimaginable. Nevertheless, I must say that I would find such a mute, gloomy, dry, doomed son unbearable, if there were no other option, I would no doubt flee from him, emigrate, as you meant to do only because of my marriage. So this may also have an influence on my inability to marry.

What is much more important in all this, however, is the anxiety about me. That is to be understood as follows: I have already indicated that in my writing and in everything connected with it I have made small attempts at independence and escape with the smallest success, they will hardly lead any further, many things confirm this for me. Even so, it is my duty, or rather my life consists in watching over them, not allowing any danger that I can avert, indeed no possibility of such a danger, to get at them. Marriage presents the possibility of such a danger, though also the possibility of the greatest support, but for me it is enough that there is the possibility of a danger. What would I do if it did turn out to be a danger? How could I continue living in matrimony in the perhaps undemonstrable but nonetheless irrefutable feeling of this danger? Faced with this I may waver but the final outcome is certain: I must renounce. The simile of the bird in the hand and two in the bush fits here only very remotely. I have nothing in the hand, everything is in the bush, and yet – thus decide the conditions of battle and the pressing needs of life – I must choose the nothing. It was similar with choosing my profession.

The most important obstacle to marriage, however, is the already ineradicable conviction that what is essential to the support of a family and especially to its guidance is what I've recognized in you, and indeed everything rolled into one, the good and the bad, as it is organically

combined in you, namely strength and the mocking of others, health and a certain excessiveness, eloquence and inadequacy, self-confidence and dissatisfaction with everyone else, worldly sovereignty and tyranny, knowledge of human nature and mistrust of most, then also good points without any drawbacks, such as diligence, endurance, presence of mind and fearlessness. By comparison, I had almost nothing of all this or only very little, and on this basis I dared to want to marry when I saw for myself that even you had to struggle hard in marriage and, where the children were concerned, even failed? Of course, I didn't expressly ask myself this question and didn't answer it expressly, otherwise the usual thinking about the matter would have taken over and shown me other men who are different from you (to name one close at hand who is very different from you: Uncle Richard[24]) and yet have married and have at least not collapsed under the strain, which is in itself quite something and would have been quite enough for me. But I didn't ask this question, rather I experienced it from childhood on. I tested myself not only with respect to marriage, but with respect to every trifle; with respect to every trifle you convinced me by your example and your method of upbringing, as I have tried to describe, of my incompetence, and as it was true of every trifle and put you in the right, it had, of course, to be true of the greatest thing of all, marriage. Up to the time of my marriage attempts I grew up more or less like a businessman who lives from day to day with anxieties and forebodings but without keeping precise accounts. He makes a few small profits, which he constantly fondles and ex-

---

[24] Almost all the brothers and half-brothers of Kafka's mother remained unmarried and were regarded as unworldly eccentrics; the exception was Richard Löwy, who was equally successful as a father and a businessman.

aggerates in his imagination because of their rarity, but otherwise he has only daily losses. Everything is recorded but never balanced. Now comes the necessity for balance, that is, the attempt at marriage. And with the large sums that he has to account for here, it is as if there had never been even the smallest profit, everything a single, great liability. And now marry without going mad!

This is how my life with you has been up to now and these are the prospects it holds for the future.

If you examine the grounds for the fear I have of you, you might answer: "You claim I am making things easy for myself by explaining my relationship to you simply as being your fault, but I think that in spite of your outward effort you make things not more difficult for yourself but much more rewarding. At first you reject all guilt and responsibility, in this our methods are the same. But while I attribute the sole guilt to you as frankly as I mean it, you want to be simultaneously 'overly clever' and 'overly affectionate' and acquit me also of all guilt. Of course, you only appear to succeed with the latter (you don't really want more), and what is revealed between the lines, in spite of all 'the turns of phrase' about character and nature and conflict and helplessness, is that actually I have been the aggressor, while everything that you did was only self-defense. By now you would have achieved enough by your insincerity, for you have proven three things: first, you are not guilty; second, that I am guilty; and, third, that you are prepared, out of sheer magnanimity, not only to forgive me but, what is both more and less, also to prove and be willing to believe that I, contrary to the truth, however, am also not guilty. That ought to be enough for you now, but it isn't enough yet. You have namely got it into your head to live entirely off me. I admit that we fight with each other, but there are two kinds of battle. The chivalrous battle, in which independent opponents match their strengths, every man for himself, losing for himself, winning for himself. And then there is the battle of vermin, which not only sting but on top of it suck your blood to sustain their own life. That is what the real professional soldier is and that is what you are. Unable to cope with life you are, but to make it comfortable for yourself, worry-free and without self-reproaches, you prove that I have taken all your ability to cope away from you and put it into my pocket. What does it matter to you now if you are unable to cope with life, since I am responsible for it, you just calmly stretch out and let yourself be hauled through life, physically and mentally, by me. One example: When you recently wanted to marry, you wanted – and you do admit it in this letter – at the same time not to marry, but so as not to have to exert yourself, you wanted me to help you with this not marrying, by forbidding this marriage because of the 'shame' this union would bring upon my name. But this didn't even occur to me. First, in this as in everything else, I never wanted 'to be an obstacle to your happiness' and, second, I don't ever want to have to hear such a reproach from my child. But did the self-restraint with which I left the marriage up to you do me any good? Not in the least. My aversion to your marriage would not have prevented it; on the contrary, it would have been even more of an incentive for you to marry the girl, for it would have made the 'attempt at escape,' as you express it, complete. And my consent to your marriage did not prevent your reproaches, for you prove that it is I who am to blame for your not marrying. Basically, you have proved to me in this, as in everything else, nothing more than that all my reproaches were justified and that one more particularly justified charge was still missing, namely the charge of insincerity, toadying, parasitism. If I am not terribly mistaken, you are sponging off me even with this letter itself."

To this I answer that, first of all, this entire objection, which can partly also be turned against you, does not come from you, but from me. Not even your distrust of others is as great as my distrust of myself, which you have reared in me. I do not deny a certain justification for this objection, which in itself also contributes to the characterization of our relationship. Naturally, in reality things cannot fit together the way the evidence does in my letter, life is more than a jigsaw puzzle; but with the correction that arises out of this objection, a correction that I neither can nor want to explain in detail, in my opinion something so very near the truth has been achieved that it can calm us both a little and make our living and dying easier.

Franz

Afterword

Who was Franz Kafka? Not only as an author, that is, the image one gets of him by reading his literary works, but as a person? To answer this question we have to rely on the texts: on Kafka's self-portrayal and on the reports of those who knew him and wrote about him. This was above all Max Brod, Kafka's discoverer, sponsor, and close friend, and the executor of his estate, who in Prague in 1937 published his Kafka biography, which has since been translated into many languages. It was also Max Brod who, on the basis of his personal association with Kafka, immediately expressed critical doubts that an authentic picture of his personality could be gained by studying his works and autobiographical accounts.

Probably the most important of these accounts is the Letter to Father, *which Kafka wrote in November 1919 and which his father, Hermann Kafka, for whatever reason, never saw. In 1937 several passages became accessible to the public for the first time, within the framework of Brod's biography. The whole letter first appeared in 1953 as part of Kafka's collected works. Brod included it after some hesitation, yet quite rightly, as belonging to Kafka's literary oeuvre, although at the same time he assessed it as a private letter. Brod's editorial conflict is symptomatic of the difficulties that lie in trying to separate Kafka's literary work from his autobiographical work. If Brod and, likely following him, Deleuze and Guattari note or even criticize the tendency to exaggerate in the letter, then they are describing a feature of the text that generally belongs to the characteristic features of Kafka's lit-*

erary style. By exaggerating, Kafka created grotesque and even comical-caricaturish distortions and so deformed perceptible reality, to make it more discernible. "To assert myself even a little against you," he typically says in the letter, "and partly out of a kind of vengefulness, I soon began to observe, collect and exaggerate ridiculous little things that I noticed about you." A small example typical of Kafka's way of making the respect-craving representatives of social power laughable and implausible in his work had already been provided in the letter itself, in the reproach that his father did not himself abide by the rules that he imposed on his son: "At the table we were only allowed to eat, but you cleaned and clipped your fingernails, sharpened pencils, cleaned your ears with a toothpick."

The length of the letter alone, just over one hundred handwritten pages, indicates that the originally planned private and much shorter letter had, in the process of writing, turned into an ambitious literary indictment of his father, and probably not least for this reason was withheld from its addressee. The letter consists of two portraits that are mutually illuminating and which stand in contrast to one another: a self-portrait and a portrait of his father. Kafka characterizes himself with features that stand in opposition to those he attributes to his father. The father: an immensely energetic, vital, strong and self-confident man; the son: weak, incapable of living, sickly, lacking self-confidence, tormented by permanent feelings of guilt and anxiety. "I was skinny, weakly, slight; you were strong, tall, broad." The letter is to a large extent structured by such comparisons: "Compare the two of us: I, to put it very briefly, a Löwy [the mother's maiden name] with a certain Kafka foundation that, however, just isn't set in motion by the Kafka will to life, business, and conquest, but by a Löwy spur that operates more secretively, more timidly, and in a different direction, and which often fails to work at all. You, on the other hand, a true Kafka in strength, health, appetite, loudness of voice, eloquence, self-satisfaction, worldly superiority, stamina, presence of mind." The father is tyrannical, moody, extroverted, robust and unscrupulous; the *son, in contrast, is an introverted hypochondriac:* "All that occupied my mind was a concern for myself, and this in various ways. There was, for instance, the concern about my health; it started easily enough, now and then there arose a little anxiety about my digestion, my loss of hair, a spinal curvature and so on, increasing in innumerable gradations, finally ending in a real illness. But since there was nothing at all I was certain of ... naturally I became unsure of even the things nearest to me, my own body. I grew very tall but didn't know what to do with my height, the burden was too great, my back became bent; I hardly dared to move, let alone excercise, I remained weak; I regarded everything I still had at my command as a miracle, for instance, my good digestion; that sufficed to lose it, and with that the way was open to every form of hypochondria; until finally, under the superhuman effort of wanting to marry (of this I shall speak later), blood came from the lung."

Being married belongs to the features that fundamentally distinguish the father from his adult son. Kafka describes his misgivings about his wedding, which is, according to his words, "the utmost a human being can succeed in doing at all," *to show his awareness of the characteristics that his father possesses but he himself lacks.* "The most important obstacle to marriage, however, is the already ineradicable conviction that what is essential to the support of a family and especially to its guidance is what I've recognized in you, and indeed everything rolled into one, the good and the bad, as they are organically combined in you, namely strength and the mocking of others, health and a certain excessiveness, eloquence and inadequacy, self-confidence and dissatisfaction with everyone else, worldly sovereignty and tyranny, knowledge of human nature and mistrust of most, then also good points without any drawbacks such as diligence, endurance, presence of mind, and fearlessness. By comparison, I had almost nothing of all this or only very little."

The image that Kafka presents of himself in the letter, as in many other letters and in his diaries, does not, in certain passages, lack a comic element; it is a literary, extremely stylized image and does not correspond to the impression his personal appearance left on others. He notices such discrepancies himself and repeatedly picks them out as a central theme. In the process of being put on paper, Kafka's self-portrayal seemed to take on a virtually compulsive dynamic whose outcome led him to continually make corrections. But he was not the only one to do so. Brod especially made those kinds of corrections in his biography. He correctly emphasized the fabricated parts of the letter and Kafka's tendency to exaggerate, but certainly without recognizing the elements which made it a literary work: "The person close to him had in any case a different image of him than that of a man hounded by the father image: he had an image of form, willingness to create and skill, thirst for knowledge, curiosity about life, the glowingly vibrant love of people." And: "There was nothing anyone meeting Kafka would detect of some kind of burden from compulsive, gloomy impressions of youth, decadence or snobbishness, which could easily have presented themselves as ways out of such depression, such remorse of the soul. What is set down in the Letter to Father *appeared on the outside not to exist – or revealed itself rather only by way of hints and only to very close friends. I only gradually got to know and understand this grief. Kafka was, on first impression, a healthy, young person, though oddly quiet, watchful, reserved. Intellectually, he by no means went in the direction of the interestingly ailing, bizarre, grotesque, but to the greatness of nature, the healing, the medicinal, the healthy, the solidly structured, the simple. I have experienced again and again that Kafka's admirers, who only know him from his books, have a completely false impression of him. They believe he must have seemed sad, even desperate, with aquaintances. The opposite is the case."*

There are several reasons to distrust even Brod's characterization of Kafka, at least in the details. And there have been many objections made to them, too. In doing so, critics have overlooked the time and the ideological-political situation in which Brod published his Kafka biography. If in 1937 he had wanted to free Kafka – whose work still had to gain acceptance – of the odium of the morbid and decadent, if he emphasized what a "good horseman, swimmer and rower" he felt Kafka to be, if he stressed Kafka's joy at everything that was "healthy and evolved" and his lack of interest in "authors of the 'dark side' and decadence," it must be viewed as a defence of Kafka, four years after the National Socialist seizure of power, against the Nazi condemnations of decadence and degeneration with which its totalitarian cultural politics resisted modernist literature.

However, Brod's doubt that an authentic portrait of Kafka's personality can be gained from his literary and autobiographical portrayals remains correct. Whoever writes is alone and therefore always in a different situation than being in the company of others. Kafka himself was well aware of his tendency to exaggerate when describing his depressing situations. During the night of February 13, 1913, he asked Felice Bauer to speak truthfully about every uneasy feeling. "You see," he added, "I don't at all require that you exaggerate for the worse, or that the exaggeration is transparent, as I – though less out of consideration for you and much more because of my nature – regularly do."

The letter to his father provides a good example of this. It is very much a self-portrait and autobiographical document. It is unsuitable to serve as a literary or psychological explanation of his stories and novels of biographical facts because it is itself literature. With the letter Kafka took up a multitude of themes and motifs that are also characteristic of his fictional texts: anxiety and guilt, accusations and condemnations, freedom and power, artistry and profession, sexuality. A key concept in the letter, as in his complete works, is "struggle." Kafka's works are to a great extent descriptions of a struggle – a struggle for and against power. What Elias Canetti wrote about Kafka in 1968 directs us to the heart of his writings: "Kafka is, of all writers, the greatest expert in power. He has experienced and shaped it in each of its aspects."

The painting of two contrasting human portraits in this long letter, that of the strong father and the weak son, goes far beyond individual character sketches and descriptions of personal family conflicts. The father-son conflict is quite similar in Vienna, Munich or Berlin to what it is in Prague. It is a standard theme of the expressionist generation as it is of psychoanalysis, still young at the time, and it stands at the centre of its struggles with representatives and institutions of social power. The "protest against the fathers," wrote the expressionist writer Rudolf Kayser in 1918 about Walter Hasenclever's play The Son, *one year before Kafka's letter was written, "is a protest against the inhibiting of the young by state, society and family." The conflict between fathers and sons merely formed a vivid model for the variety of conflicts, every now and then reaching deep into the unconscious, between the individual and the authorities and powers of a patriarchically organized society. With it Kafka embraces psychological and social, legal and pedagogic, political and religious aspects simultaneously.*

An important figure, eminent in this context (a figure who actually existed but was also fictionalized and keeps reappearing in the stories, novels and dramas of the expressionists), was the unorthodox student of Freud, Otto Gross. Kafka, like many other writers of the expressionist generation, felt closely linked to him for a time. The "most important student of Sigmund Freud," according to Munich anarchist Erich Mühsam, imparted psychoanalysis in a cultural-revolutionary version to the literary and bohemian circles in Munich, Ascona, Berlin, Vienna and Prague.

Even if Kafka did not propagate the revolutionary struggle "against rape in its original form, against the father and patriarchy," at least not as openly and resolutely as Gross did, there are several points of contact between the literary analyses of power, dependency, guilt and impotence of the one and the theoretical analyses of the other. And even the personal experiences that stand behind them apparently had some similarities.

"Somebody must have slandered Otto G., for he was arrested one morning without having done anything wrong." As in The Trial, *so too could a story about that sensational case in Berlin in November 1913 begin, about nine months before Kafka started writing his novel. The well-known and influential professor of criminal law Hans Gross had his son Otto, who had broken out of the bourgeois order, abducted by the Berlin police and taken to an Austrian lunatic asylum, supposedly for being "mentally ill, and constituting a public danger." Kafka knew of this affair. Several expressionist writers, who had here before their very eyes a most real example for their literary motif of the father-son conflict, initiated a protest campaign. It generated such a response that the compulsory institutionalization was soon lifted.*

Kafka was a reader of the Berlin expressionist magazine Die Aktion, *which published some essays by Gross. Here, too, the scandal was often referred to; a special issue was even devoted to it. Kafka must have become aware of this case because he knew Gross' father from his study of law. For three semesters he was enrolled in Hans Gross' lectures in Prague, where the latter taught at the time.*

Kafka got to know Otto Gross personally in July 1917 during an overnight train trip from Budapest to Prague. The Viennese writer Anton Kuh, a brother-in-law of Gross', was also present. It must have been an odd journey. Kuh, as Kafka tells Milena Jesenska, "sang and made noise half the night," while Gross expounded his theory to him. Still in the same month they both met in Brod's apartment. Brod gave a brief account of it later in his Kafka biography: "On 23 July I had a lot of company which included, besides Kafka, the musician Adolf Schreiber, Werfel, Otto Gross and his wife, and Gross was developing plans for a magazine, which interested Kafka very much." Kafka's own recollection, four months later, sounded far more enthusiastic. He wrote Brod, "If a magazine seemed tempting to me for a long time (at the moment, naturally all of them do), then it was that of Dr. Gross because it seemed to me, at least on that evening, to come out of the fire of a cer-

tain personal closeness. A sign of an effort which involves being personally bound together, more than that perhaps a magazine cannot be."

It was to be called Pages for the Struggle for Power. *It never appeared; still, the "fire of a certain personal closeness" to Gross left behind clear traces in later works, especially in* Letter to Father *and in the fragment of the novel* The Castle. *"Struggle" and "power," two terms from the title of the planned magazine, are now even more dominant than in Kafka's earlier texts. The letter not only picks up as a central theme the struggle of the son against the patriarchal power of the father, but it is itself an instrument in this battle in which the father, as he is portrayed in the letter, has something in common with the father of Gross. Both were social Darwinists of the most dubious sort. The expert in criminal law had distinguished himself in diverse writings with arguments calling for the deportation of biologically inferior and, in the struggle for existence, unsuitable criminals to the colonies of southwest Africa for the sake of the health of society. Kafka's story "In the Penal Colony," written in the early months of the First World War, is inadequately understood without the knowledge of such treatises and practices. Kafka's father, who in the letter embodies the social Darwinist virtues of strength and robust health and represents them with his words, thinks in similar categories as Hans Gross does. The weakly son is in his eyes a vermin unfit for independent life. "I admit," so Kafka allows his father himself to have a word at the end, "that we fight with each other, but there are two kinds of battle. The chivalrous battle, in which independent opponents match their strengths.... And then there is the battle of vermin, which not only sting but on top of it suck your blood to sustain their own life." The father's judgement of the son is: "Unable to cope with life you are." Over and above that the son has tuberculosis – as is the case with an employee of his father's about whom he once said: "Let him croak, the sick dog." Apart from that, the son associates, as does Gross, with "crazy friends" and works on "extravagant ideas." In his* works Hans Gross had written in a similar tone characterizing the degenerate, and therefore fit only to be deported, outsiders of society, about the "sexually perverse," "eternally dissatisfied," "subversive," "players at professions," "mentally ill" and the like, in other words about a social type with whom those in expressionist circles sympathized.

At issue in Kafka's seemingly private examination of his powerful father is the above-mentioned social Darwinism, which had at the time become the universal ideology justifying social and political power struggles and which, in the name of evolutionary progress, had championed the basic right of the stronger in the struggle for existence. According to the letter, the father owes his position of power to a battle fought since childhood, a battle from which he emerged victorious. "What you'd had to fight for we received from your hand; but the fight for external life, a fight that was instantly accessible to you, and which we are, of course, not spared either, we have to fight later, as adults with the strength of a child."

The father's triumphantly gained power reaches beyond the family; it is also the "power of the boss" toward the employees of his firm. The letter chooses economic structures as well as family structures as central themes. And just as the interpersonal relationships are labeled by recurring terms such as "struggle," "supremacy" and "estrangement" in Kafka's representation of the family, so also in the powerfully critical description of the "business" is the relationship between employer and personnel identified: "You called your employees 'paid enemies,' and this they were, but even before they became that you seemed to me to be their 'paying enemy.' There, too, I learned the great lesson that you could be unjust; in my case I would not have noticed it so soon for I had accumulated too many feelings of guilt, which made me ready to agree with you; but in my childish opinion – later, of course, somewhat modified, although not all too much so – there were strangers in the shop who nevertheless worked for us, and because of this had to live in perpetual fear of you.

Of course I exaggerated, because I simply assumed that you had just as terrible an effect on those people as on me. If that had been the case, they could not have been able to live at all; but since they were adults with mostly excellent nerves, they effortlessly shook off your abuse and in the end it did you much more harm than it did them. For me, however, it made the shop intolerable, it reminded me far too much of my relationship to you: you were, quite apart from your entrepreneurial interest and apart from your need to be domineering, even as a businessman so greatly superior to all those who ever trained with you that none of their accomplishments could ever satisfy you, and you must similarly have been forever dissatisfied with me, too. That's why I necessarily took the side of the staff."

In his letter Kafka organized his description of his relationship to his father systematically, according to several problem areas, all of which play an important part in his work: upbringing, business, Judaism, his existence as a writer, occupation, sexuality and marriage. There is a place in the letter which expressly emphasizes the universal significance of what is being portrayed. It is in the section where his father's merely superficial and indifferent attitude to Judaism is addressed, by which the raising of his son in the spirit of Jewish traditions became insubstantial and implausible. "The whole thing is, of course, no isolated phenomenon," he writes. "It was much the same with a large portion of this transitional generation of Jews which migrated from the comparatively still pious countryside to the cities." The son acquits his father of guilt "in this point too" and asks his father to account for this blamelessness not by personal circumstances but "by the circumstances of the time."

The letter is in any case less about personal circumstances than about the "circumstances of the time." The era in which it was written was the post-war and revolutionary era. A few months before Kafka wrote his letter, an essay – separately published in the same year – appeared in the magazine Der österreichische Volkswirt *[the Austrian Economist]* *(May*

1919) with the title "On the Psychology of the Revolution: the Fatherless Society." The psychoanalyst Paul Federn tried to show here to what extent the old authoritarian imperial state had its foundation in the "desire for father-like authority" that had its origins in patriarchal family relationships, and that the "fall of the emperor" necessitated a change in the traditional family structure. Kafka's letter contains no explicit references to the political conflicts of the time, but his vocabulary acquires an eminently political dimension when "spiritual supremacy," "the exercise of power," or "violence and overthrow" are discussed. And when he says of his father, "From your easychair you ruled the world," or, "For me, you took on that enigmatic something that all tyrants have whose law is founded on their person, not their reasoning."

Certainly Kafka was not, in any concrete sense, a political author. With regard to the great political events of his time (world war and revolution) he rather showed a disconcerting ignorance. He noted the beginning of the war on August 2, 1914, with the succinct diary entry: "Germany has declared war on Russia. – In afternoon swimming school." Of his interest in writing he noted four days later, not without self-criticism: "From the point of view of literature my destiny is quite simple. The desire to portray my dreamlike inner life has pushed everything else to the periphery, and it has, in a terrible way, withered away and does not cease to wither away." First and foremost, fantasies of guilt and punishment stand out in his literary representations of his inner life. In the second week of August he started work on The Trial; *in October the story "In the Penal Colony" appeared. In the* Letter to Father *guilt is a permanent topic of discussion: "I had lost my self-confidence where you were concerned, had traded it for a boundless sense of guilt. (In recollection of this boundlessness I once wrote of someone, accurately, 'He is afraid the shame will outlive him')." The (inaccurate) self-citation is taken from the end of* The Trial, *in which Josef K. obligingly allows himself to be executed. Of course, the letter does not supply any biographical explanations for this novel, but instead falls back on its own literary court imagery: He speaks of the "terrible trial that hovers between us and you," of a trial "in which you continue to claim to be the judge." The letter communicates a very clear recognition that the son's boundless feelings of guilt (as with his anxiety) are the result (formulated with Gross) of the "father's authority which has penetrated into his inner being, that the struggle with one's father continues deep inside as a struggle 'between the self and the alien.'" "Between us there was no real struggle; I was soon finished off; what remained was ... inner struggle." With a tremendously subtle literary technique the letter again demonstrates this process of the internalization of paternal power. He lets his father formulate a possible response to the letter, which culminates in "the charge of insincerity, toadying, parasitism. If I am not terribly mistaken, you are sponging off me even with this letter itself." But these charges are not articulated by a real father but by the imaginary father in the mind of his son; consequently they are self-reproaches. The letter says so explicitly. The son responds to his father's invented objections to the letter: "To this I answer that, after all, this entire objection ... does not come from you but from me. Not even your distrust of others is as great as my distrust of myself which you have reared in me. I do not deny a certain justification for this objection."*

"There is a general mobilization," noted Kafka in his diary on July 31, 1914, and at the end of his entry defines his writing as a "struggle for self-preservation." A few days after starting work on The Trial *he notes, relieved, "I can have a dialogue with myself again." As with the novel, the letter is later a struggle for self-assertion fought out with his father, and an inner dialogue with him, and finally also a kind of court trial in which, during an era of escalating class, race and other competitive struggles, the guilt is negotiated regarding the struggle for which the family relationships have become perverted. The writer of the letter acts the defendant in the father's "incessant charges," as his own defence attorney, and as an author who finds, at least in writing, the strength to*

oppose his father as prosecutor and judge. The charges against his father are vehement; the evidence for his weaknesses, contradictions and "absurdities," found by the hyperacute observations of his son, severely dismantles his authority. That he himself did not keep the commandments he imposed on his son is only one example of his illegitimate usurpation of power. That he did not encourage, or at least respect, his son's unique individuality (incidentally, his daughter's too), but instead suppressed it, is the main point of the accusation, with which all the others are integrated: "I would have needed a little encouragement, a little friendliness, a little keeping open of my path, instead you obstructed it for me, with the good intention, it is true, of making me take a different path. But for that I was useless." The letter describes the consequences of this ignorance with respect to his "real existence" in several ways, including the following: "I lost confidence in my own ability to act. I was unsteady, doubtful. The older I got, the more material you could hold against me as proof of my worthlessness; gradually, in a certain regard, you began really to be right. Once again I guard against claiming that I became like this only because of you; you only reinforced what was there, but you reinforced it greatly because you were very powerful in relation to me and you used all your power for that purpose."

Despite such accusations, the trial, as it is stage-managed in the letter, is directed from the beginning at a settlement, at a peace offer in the battle of a social micro-organism. The father had "partly caused" the broken family relations, "but without blame." The son exculpates his father and wants for his part to be acquitted by him: "I also believe that you are entirely blameless regarding our estrangement. But just as entirely blameless am I. If I could get you to acknowledge this, then what would be possible is not a new life – for this we are both much too old – but still a kind of peace, not a cessation but still a mitigation of your incessant reproaches." What the letter states as a goal, a "sort of peace" between the fighters, it describes two more times: once as an unattainable utopia and, at the end, as the possible result of gaining literary recognition.

The letter concludes in a conciliatory tone, saying, "In my opinion something so very near the truth has been achieved that it can calm us both a little and make our living and dying easier."

Thomas Anz*

---

* Thomas Anz is professor of modern German literary studies at the University of Bamberg. The afterword is based on his book *Franz Kafka*, 2nd ed. (Munich: Beck, 1992).